YAKS

WILLOW CLARK

PowerKiDS press™

New York

Published in 2013 by The Rosen Publishing Group, Inc.
29 East 21st Street, New York, NY 10010

First Edition

Editor: Joanne Randolph
Book Design: Ashley Drago

Photo Credits: Cover, pp. 5 (right), 8, 9, 10, 11(top and bottom), 13 (top),17 Shutterstock.com; pp. 4, 7, 22 Hemera/Thinkstock.com; pp. 5 (left), 20 © www.iStockphoto.com/Bartosz Hadyniak; p. 12 © www.iStockphoto.com/Irina Efremova; p. 13 (left) Travel Ink/Gallo Images/Getty Images; pp. 13, 21 © www.iStockphoto.com/Alexander Semenov; p. 14 Jane Sweeney/Robert Harding World Imagery/Getty Images; p. 15 Keren Su/China Span/Getty Images; p. 18 Tom Brakefield/Stockbyte/Getty Images; p. 19 Gayle Dickson/Flickr Open/Getty Images.

Library of Congress Cataloging-in-Publication Data

Clark, Willow.
 Yaks / by Willow Clark. — 1st ed.
    p. cm. — (The animals of Asia)
 Includes index.
 ISBN 978-1-4488-7415-6 (library binding) — ISBN 978-1-4488-7488-0 (pbk.) —
ISBN 978-1-4488-7562-7 (6-pack)
 1. Yak—Juvenile literature. I. Title.
 QL737.U53C59 2013
 599.64'22—dc23
                              2011050664

Manufactured in China
CPSIA Compliance Information: Batch #WKTS12PK: For Further Information contact Rosen Publishing, New York, New York at 1-800-237-9932

CONTENTS

HELLO, YAK!..4

A MOUNTAIN ANIMAL 6

KEEPING COOL 8

THE YAK'S FUR...10

HORNS AND HOOVES 12

PART OF THE HERD...14

WHAT'S FOR LUNCH? 16

WATCH OUT, YAK! 18

BABY YAKS 20

WILD YAKS IN TROUBLE 22

GLOSSARY 23

INDEX 24

WEBSITES..24

HELLO, YAK!

The yak is an animal that belongs to the same scientific family as cows and bison. Like bison, yaks have shaggy hair that helps keep them warm in their cold **habitat**.

These yaks live in Mongolia, where winter temperatures can be as low as -22° F (-30° C). ▼

People in Tibet have raised yaks for thousands of years. They use yaks to help them do work. They also use the milk, fibers, and even the dung of the yak.

Yaks' habitat is cold and snowy much of the year. Yaks have no trouble climbing steep mountain slopes as they look for food.

There are both wild and **domestic** yaks. Domestic yaks are smaller than wild yaks. They are used to do farmwork, kept for their milk and meat, and their hair is used to make wool. Today, domestic yaks are plentiful, but the number of wild yaks is falling. This book will explain why and teach you about this Asian animal.

A MOUNTAIN ANIMAL

Wild yaks live in northern India and the Tibetan Plateau. The Tibetan Plateau includes the regions of Tibet, Gansu, Qinghai, and Xinjiang, in China. Wild yaks once lived in Nepal and Bhutan, too. Today they are considered **extinct** in these countries because they do not live there anymore.

WHERE YAKS LIVE

This map shows where in Asia yaks live.
▼

Mongolia

China

PACIFIC OCEAN

India

KEY

Yak range

▲ *Yaks live in alpine meadows, alpine steppes, and desert steppes. A steppe is a grassland without many trees.*

The Tibetan Plateau is a high plain surrounded by mountain ranges. It has an average **elevation** of about 14,800 feet (4,500 m). This elevation is so high that it earned the plateau and the surrounding mountains a nickname. They are called the roof of the world.

KEEPING COOL

The wild yak's habitat ranges from mountainous **tundra**, to mountain meadows, to cold deserts. The climate in these places is often cold and dry. Not much grows in this climate except grasses, mosses, and lichens. These make up a large part of the yak's diet.

There are not a lot of food choices where yaks live. This is part of the reason why wild yaks are in trouble. Domesticated yak herds eat food that wild yaks need to live.

Yaks **migrate** with the seasons. In the winter, they often come to lower elevations where more vegetation is growing. As the weather warms in the summer, they move back up to where it is colder. Yaks do not like hot weather, but they can stand temperatures that are colder than -40° F (-40° C)!

Yaks' thick fur keeps them warm in the snow. Yaks start overheating once temperatures get to around 60° F (15° C).

THE YAK'S FUR

The wild yak has a big body. Its can be up to 11 feet (3 m) long and stand up to 6 feet (2 m) tall at its humped shoulders. It weighs up to 1,800 pounds (820 kg). The domestic yak is smaller. Both

Yaks have longer fur on top of their heads, along the bottom of their bodies, and on their tails.

Here you can see this yak's long fur, humped back, and curved horns. The fur on a yak can grow so long that it forms a skirt around the yak's legs. ▶

wild and domestic female yaks weigh one-third to one-half as much as males.

The yak's fur is long, thick, and shaggy. In the winter, yaks grow short, thick undercoats that keep them warm. The wild yak's fur is dark brown or black. Domestic yaks can have red, brown, black, or multicolored fur.

◀ While wild yaks are generally brown or black, domestic yaks can be white or spotted, too.

HORNS AND HOOVES

The yak's horns and hooves are **adaptations** that help the animal live well in its habitat. Both male and female yaks have curved horns. The male's horns can be up to twice as long as the female's horns, though. The horns are hard and

Domesticated yaks are generally smaller than wild yaks. They have shorter legs and horns and broader hooves, too.

Yaks, like cows and bison, are part of a group called even-toed ungulates. Ungulates are animals with hooves. ▶

strong. Yaks use them to break through snow and ice so they can graze on the plants underneath.

Yaks might look like big, awkward animals. The yak's short legs and wide hooves allow it to climb snowy, rocky slopes without slipping, though. Yaks also use their hard hooves to dig for food.

◀ The horns on male yaks can be up to 39 inches (99 cm) long. Horns on the female are shorter and can be up to 25 inches (64 cm) long.

13

PART OF THE HERD

Like their cow cousins, yaks often travel together in groups called herds. A herd can have from 10 to more than 100 yaks. The herd is made up of mostly females and their young and very few adult males. Forming a herd helps protect the young from **predators**.

Male yaks sometimes form small herds with other males. During mating season, though, males may sometimes fight each other.

The herd is not a fixed group. Smaller herds sometimes come together for a while. Larger herds may split into smaller groups. Adult male yaks sometimes leave the herd to graze on their own. At other times, they form small groups with other adult males. This kind of group is called a bachelor herd.

A herd of yaks

15

WHAT'S FOR LUNCH?

Yaks are **herbivores**. This means that they eat only plants. They graze on the grasses, shrubs, mosses, lichens, and other vegetation that grows in their habitat.

Like their cow cousins, yaks have a special way to digest, or break down, their food. First, they swallow their food without chewing it. After one part of their stomachs breaks down the food a little bit, the partly digested food, or cud, goes back into the mouth. The yak then chews, swallows, and digests the cud. This special way of eating allows yaks to get all of the **nutrients** they can out of the food they eat.

Yaks eat less than cows do. It still takes a lot of plant matter to feed a yak, though! ▶

WATCH OUT, YAK!

The main predator of both wild yaks and domestic yaks is the Tibetan wolf. This is a type of wolf found throughout central Asia. Other, less common yak predators are snow leopards and

Snow leopards are one of the top predators in southern and central Asia. Just as the yak is, the snow leopard is adapted to life high up in the cold, snowy mountains.

▼

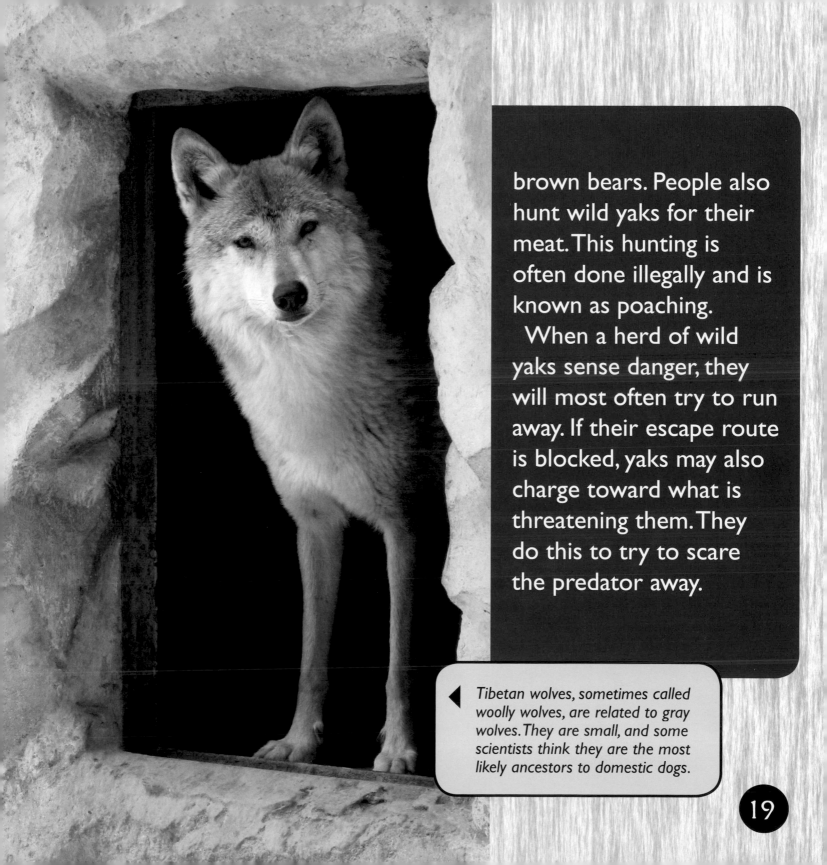

brown bears. People also hunt wild yaks for their meat. This hunting is often done illegally and is known as poaching.

When a herd of wild yaks sense danger, they will most often try to run away. If their escape route is blocked, yaks may also charge toward what is threatening them. They do this to try to scare the predator away.

Tibetan wolves, sometimes called woolly wolves, are related to gray wolves. They are small, and some scientists think they are the most likely ancestors to domestic dogs.

BABY YAKS

The wild yak's **mating** season starts in September and lasts for a few weeks. During that time, male yaks will look for female herds. The males will fight each other for the chance to mate with females.

Wild yak babies are about 40 pounds (18 kg) when they are born. Domestic yaks are a bit smaller. Both wild and domestic yak babies grow quickly, though!

Male yaks do not have a role in raising calves. Females generally give birth to one calf every two years.

Baby yaks, or calves, are generally born in June. The calves can stand and walk within a few hours after being born. Mothers **nurse** and care for their calves for about a year, after which a young yak is big enough to take care of itself. Yaks are full-grown adults at around six to eight years of age. The wild yak's life span is about 20 years.

WILD YAKS IN TROUBLE

Wild yaks are considered a **vulnerable species**. That is because their numbers have dropped by about one-third over the past 30 years. One of the threats to wild yaks is habitat loss caused by the spread of farms with herds of livestock. Wild yaks will move away from places where people and livestock live.

Another threat to wild yaks is poaching. Laws in China and India now protect wild yaks. It is hoped that better enforcement of these laws will keep the wild yak safe from becoming endangered or extinct.

Interestingly, the livestock that is crowding out wild yaks is often herds of domestic yaks!

GLOSSARY

ADAPTATIONS (a-dap-TAY-shunz) Changes in animals that help them stay alive.

DOMESTIC (duh-MES-tik) Having to do with animals made by people choosing which animals to breed together.

ELEVATION (eh-luh-VAY-shun) The height of an object.

EXTINCT (ik-STINGKT) No longer existing.

HABITAT (HA-buh-tat) The kind of land where an animal or a plant naturally lives.

HERBIVORES (ER-buh-vorz) Animals that eat only plants.

MATING (MAYT-ing) Coming together to make babies.

MIGRATE (MY-grayt) To move from one place to another.

NURSE (NURS) When a female feeds her baby milk from her body.

NUTRIENTS (NOO-tree-unts) Food that a living thing needs to live and grow.

PREDATORS (PREH-duh-terz) Animals that kill other animals for food.

SPECIES (SPEE-sheez) One kind of living thing. All people are one species.

TUNDRA (TUN-druh) The icy land of the coldest parts of the world.

VULNERABLE (VUL-neh-ruh-bel) Could be easily hurt.

INDEX

A
adaptations, 12

B
bison, 4

E
elevation(s), 7, 9

F
farmwork, 5

H
habitat, 4, 8, 12, 16

I
India, 6, 22

M
meat, 5, 19
mothers, 21

N
number(s), 5, 22
nutrients, 16

P
predator(s), 14, 18–19

R
regions, 6

S
scientific family, 4
season(s), 9, 20
species, 22

T
Tibet, 6
Tibetan Plateau, 6–7
tundra, 8

WEBSITES

Due to the changing nature of Internet links, PowerKids Press has developed an online list of websites related to the subject of this book. This site is updated regularly. Please use this link to access the list: www.powerkidslinks.com/aoa/yaks/